In the Big Apple the snow is falling down, and the chilly air is swirling all around.

But the streets are buzzing with Holiday Cheer, as Christmastime is finally here!

The shops on 5th Avenue are all aglow, with twinkling lights and windows full of snow.

At Rockefeller Center, children marvel at the tree. So festive, bright, and grand to see.

The Union Square Holiday Market is a sight to behold, where Christmas themed treats and warm drinks are sold.

Lady Liberty covered in snow, a beacon of freedom for all to behold.

Ice skaters glide and twirl with grace,
Downtown New York, a magical place.

Macy's windows dressed up with glee, a festive scene for all to see.

Bronx Zoo, Oh what a view! The sparkling lights will dazzle you.

In Central Park the lights shine bright, sparkling with beauty on a Winter's night.

Take a stroll through Brooklyn's Dyker Heights, to witness the most festive Holiday lights.

At F.A.O. Schwarz Christmas dreams come alive.
A wonderland of toys, where imaginations will thrive.

Visit Santaland at Macy's Herald Square. Where Holiday Magic fills the air.

Head to Levain Bakery when the winter winds blow. Sip some hot chocolate nice and slow.

Horse-drawn carriage, a sight so rare, rolls down 5th Avenue with grace and flair.

With the hustle and bustle of the city below, there's a sense of warmth that all shall know.

At Central Park's Pilgrim Hill with sled in hand, race down the paths of a Winter Wonderland.

As night falls over the city, the skyline aglow, a most beautiful sight for all to behold.

A Christmas movie by the fireplace light will keep us warm on a chilly night.

Leave out milk and cookies for Santa's delight, hoping he will come on Christmas night.

And on Christmas morning we rush to the tree, to find Santa left presents for you and me!

So if you're ever in The Big Apple at Christmastime, You'll see that its beauty is truly divine.

Merry Christmas
from
New York City

www.ingramcontent.com/pod-product-compliance
Lightning Source LLC
Chambersburg PA
CBHW041557040426
42447CB00002B/210